A Families Journey with

with

Alzheimer's Disease

Bob Sh'mal
ELLENBERG

BALBOA.
PRESS

A DIVISION OF HAY HOUSE

Balboa Press books may be ordered through booksellers or by contacting:

Balboa Press
A Division of Hay House
1663 Liberty Drive
Bloomington, IN 47403
www.balboapress.com
1 (877) 407-4847

Print information available on the last page.

ISBN: 978-1-9822-2200-0 (sc)
ISBN: 978-1-9822-2201-7 (e)

Balboa Press rev. date: 02/19/2019

CONTENTS

CHAPTER 1

My Father's Problem Commences

When my mother began to complain about the difficult time she was having dealing with my 81 year old father and his Alzheimer's-like behavior, my immediate reaction was to some how, at some point, bring him to Gainesville where I lived with my children and have him live with us. Since my ex-wife and I had cared for elderly and handicapped adults in our home for 12 years, and I had been a social worker and counselor for elderly and mentally disturbed adults, I felt comfortable letting my mother and sister know I would bring my dad to Gainesville when the time was right.

But both my mother and sister were uncertain about me doing this, expressing their reservations having him move so far from our mother. In most respects I agreed with them that it was too soon to have our father make that move while leaving our

1

mother by herself in Ft. Lauderdale. I told them that the offer was open to both my parents when they wanted that move.

My parents were not wealthy by most standards. They had some money in savings, but my mother was afraid of not having money for herself when she was older, so she was reluctant to use what money they had for a change in life, such as moving to Gainesville where I could help them. I told my mother, "Mom, you are older, you're almost 80, now is the time to use your money for your care and the care of dad."

I wasn't even living in a house with my children, but sharing a house with my ex-wife on alternate weeks with the children, using a trailer on the other weeks. I would need financial help getting a house to accommodate my three kids and my dad.

I think my mother and my sister also had their doubt that I could do it. I had this feeling maybe it was even expressed, that they didn't trust me in doing this sacred work. I had never meant much to my mother because she didn't see me as a successful person. My sister may have felt the same, and I felt put down by both, because money to them was the criteria for success. They had no clue though, who I was and what determination was in me to do right by my parents. For the time being, things were on hold, as we would wait and assess; letting the future unfold.

My mother couldn't be persuaded. She was content where she was living, and wanted to see how things went for a while longer. It was naturally hard for her to give up on her husband of over 50 years. I understood the problem. My parents had many friends in the condo, they knew the movie theaters, streets, restaurants and didn't want to deal with the disruption that goes with a move. But she continued to get more and more distressed dealing with my dad's forgetfulness, odd responses during conversation, even forgetting, at times, who my mother was. He also stopped doing things he enjoyed for the almost 20 years they lived in Ft. Lauderdale. His changes were approaching being serious, but still not enough to warrant making any move yet. From my regular visits, I could see he was deteriorating, making it difficult for my mother, but to her credit, she wanted to care for him as long as she could.

My mother was never a patient woman, and she was accustomed to things being just so, with everything in its place, and now, everything was slowly coming out of its place. She liked control, especially in things they did together, and now those times were over and he wasn't being the docile husband he had been. She was being presented with problems she never thought she would have to deal with, so it was natural for her to become unsettled and agitated when her husband began exhibiting the behavior described above.

After overcoming denial, and trying as best she could with her personality, it was a slow awakening that she was less and less able to care for him.

CHAPTER 2

Finding A Place For Dad

As his odd behavior went into its second year I began pleading with my mother and my sister for financial help to get a house so I could take him in with my kids. Although we talked about a couple of ways to negotiate this, nothing seemed right to either of them. (Later on the both helped me with fixing the house.) Under the emotional strain of it all, my sister and I even exchanged some insults. I too began to feel distressed and increasing uncomfortable about myself for not being able to just do it on my own. I became annoyed at myself for not having more money, feeling weak asking for contributions from family. In the meantime my sister and mother kept suggesting a residential care home for my dad.

I had many negative feelings about placing either of my parents in nursing homes or other facilities to do the work family members did in the past. There was something deep in me, as if in my loins, mainly my conscience that made caring for my parents something natural and important. Having worked with the elderly and handicapped I was familiar with nursing homes and other care facilities. I didn't go for it; it wasn't in me. I was committed to figure out a way to take care my parents as they had done for me. In fact, I had moved to Florida with my wife and children to be closer to parents if and when they needed help. I tried to be patient, understanding the time wasn't right. I knew that since my mother didn't want to move, and naturally my father, was indifferent, actually, he had no clue, but for my mom, having him nearby, in some kind of facility, would work for the time being.

Finally dad had a couple of accidents urinating in his pants. For my mother, being a lifetime clean freak, this was almost the last straw. Then he twice walked away from their condominium getting lost and fell a couple of times, my mother realized she could no longer live with him. She asked my sister and me for help in placing him in a supervised setting. My sister flew down from New Jersey and looked at a few places, and when she left, I reluctantly, but with understanding for my mother, drove down from Gainesville and also looked at some facilities. At this point, dad didn't need skilled nursing care as in a nursing home, so we looked at care facilities.

They offer food, housekeeping, laundry and full time supervision, to one degree or another.

I knew it was important that I supported my mother fully with this decision. It was a no-brainer. We all agreed it was dangerous for dad walking off and getting lost. I reminded mom I had worked around handicapped people for years, both in my home and in mental health centers, and in time I would try and have dad come live with my kids and me. She tried to act reassured.

When I arrived in Ft. Lauderdale I could see my mother was very disturbed in making this decision. Naturally she was feeling a lot of guilt with hurt feelings in deciding she couldn't do it herself. She justified what she was doing by telling me how many people are doing it: "What's wrong with it? Why do you think they have these places?" Although I knew what I believed was "right" I assured her she needn't feel guilty: "We are making the best decision." I told her that if she wasn't able to deal with his new behaviors it was natural, "I don't want you to get sick taking care of him." I kept reassuring her, "We'll find a good place for him. I've worked with many families that go through the same thing." My social work experience was now being used for my parents. I felt that my many years of training were for this purpose.

When we went to look at places we took Dad with us so he would have some idea what was happening to his life and for the staff to interview him making sure they could handle his idiosyncrasies and his behaviors. I knew he wasn't unusual for what these care facilities normally deal with, and that he wouldn't be a problem. I made sure during our touring that he knew what we were doing in these places: "Dad, do you understand that we are looking for a place for you to live because mom can't take care of you any more?"

Typically from a man that always seemed content, he responded, "I don't care, put me where you want." I almost cried hearing him being ambivalent, maybe even a little angry. It was somewhere around this time I realized he was maybe less than content with life. It seemed like there was a combination of indifference and resignation. Not the highest of personality traits, but in some ways it made him angel-like in how he dealt with certain aspects of life. If things didn't go his way he never let it ruffle his equanimity. In his relationships with people, he always had a broad smile, with a friendly hello for those he knew and as well as for strangers. I used to joke with friends that if more people were like him, not much would get done, but we would have a peaceful world.

After looking at a few places we finally decided on one that was recommended by friends of my mother. It was called a care facility which had the same name as a resort in the Catskill Mountains in upstate New York. My father and mother used to occasionally go on vacations in the Catskills but never to this expensive resort. I didn't think it was a coincidence that this place looked like a fancy hotel, with chandeliers, plush sitting chairs in the spacious, thick carpeted, lobby, with a front desk similar to that in a hotel. I knew though that these were only the make-things-look-good amenities. The criteria for care are how many staff a place has and how well they treated their guests. I also believed if staff are treated well, than the residents will be treated the same. One only knew about these things after a person was there a while.

The amenities and trappings made my mother feel good. Much less fancy would have suited dad fine, but in some ways it was more important for mom to feel comfortable about these things than my father.

I felt frustrated in not knowing what else to do, but for the now, I went along with the family decision, agreeing it was the best thing for now. After deciding on The Caring Home I assured my sister that the place we choose was all right and they would take care of our father fine.

I had to lie to myself though, because I knew there's a real difference between being cared for by family where it is personal and one is loved versus the other. In a place with 70 or so elderly and slightly handicapped people, sometimes it's hard to get the needed attention. When there are no other alternatives, though, this is what people choose and it is what our society has to offer. I also believed that these places were only set up to make money, it just so happens they make it off of the care of others.

Fortunately, kind, caring people usually take these kinds of jobs caring for others. So I knew for dad, with his kind smile and friendly nature, it was going to be easy to win over the attention of the staff. On the other hand, I also knew that attendants working in these places, don't get paid very much and have a lot of nasty, cleaning up, busy work to do. How much care can they give day after day, night after night to all these old disabled people? After a while, in our culture, even for the most caring giving worker, it becomes more like just going to a job then a caring service to those needing love.

CHAPTER 3

Dad Moves In To Assisted Living

I accepted what was and helped move him in before I left for home. I had a little trepidation, but I left hoping it was all going to work out for him and my mother. Because my mother needed support, I committed myself to visit them every couple of months. He always appeared to be in good health, and typically for him, he didn't complain about anything. What could he complain about when he didn't know what was going on? On my visits I usually took them both out for a meal, brought him over to their apartment and spent time with them that they enjoyed. One afternoon I took dad out for a ride to the beach and walk by myself. It was a bit of a struggle to get him away from my mother, who wanted to go with us. Even when I explained to her my need to be alone with him she almost resented our bond. It felt good being out alone with him, which is something we didn't do much even when he was healthy. He seemed to be doing well. As usual he didn't say much, but in looking at him I wondered if he thought of anything, and, although something in me felt uncomfortable asking, I did, "Dad, I know you're not saying much, but are you thinking of anything?" It didn't surprise me when he simply answered, "No." I reminded him that at some point I would bring him to live with my kids and me. He always said that was fine, but I also knew he didn't remember one thing from the next.

After a few months, as I sort of anticipated, complaints began to come from my mother. That's another one of her personality traits: she's a complainer. I love her but it's true. The total opposite of dad: she's never satisfied.

"I bring him a banana or an orange, leave it in his room and it's still there when I come back in a few days; how do I know if they're washing his eye out good; I don't know if they change his clothes everyday; I have to do all the things for him anyway. I take his clothes home and wash them myself otherwise they'll get stolen; you know how they are. I don't know if they give him a shower, he says they do, but he doesn't know. They don't watch him good; he could walk out the door and get lost. He's peeing in his pants more often; who knows how often they change him?" And then, "They keep putting different men in his room, worse then he is. They're messing up the whole room.

They really don't know what they're doing." Neither did my father!

It went on and on. Both Tina and I received complaining, distressed phone calls. Dad wasn't living at home, but he was as much a worry to mom as when he was there. Maybe more since she couldn't oversee his every move. Then another unanticipated problem arose when she went to see him and found him sitting holding hands with a lady. This really upset her.

I asked mother if she was jealous. She told me she was glad he had company, "I'm not jealous. But," she said with some hurt in her voice, "the lady won't go away when I want to talk to him. He won't get up and take a walk with me. He just sits there, not saying anything, holding hands with her."

I asked her, "Would he talk or walk with you before he had the lady friend?" I knew him; he never had much to say, and for the past few years it was less and less. And walk with her? For the past few years the only place they ever walked together was in the mall. She told me what I knew, "No" she said, "he didn't walk with me."

"So, Mom, what's the difference," I asked her?

"Why do I want to go see him when he's sitting holding hands with this old lady? He doesn't even know her name. She probably doesn't know his. But they sit and hold hands. What should I do, watch them?"

"It's okay mom, they're just being friends."

She understood, she didn't understand. It was confusing and I felt compelled to do what I believed was my part. He had been there for most of a year, and it was time for me to act.

I took a chance and borrowed some money from a friend and after looking for a few months found a house I could afford in a neighborhood where my kids and I had friends. It was a bit too small, but I could fix up the garage so my 14 and 16 year-old sons could have a room. There was a bedroom for my 11 year-old daughter, Rebecca, who stayed with her mom during the week, but came to visit me on weekends; one bedroom for dad and one for me. Only thirteen hundred square feet, but it had a large backyard with a privacy fence, a lot of trees, and some space so I could peruse organic vegetable gardening. Now when I asked my sister and mom for some financial assistance to renovate the garage, they both agreed. Life really is about timing.

I needed one more change in my life to make this work right. I had a job 30 miles from home working with severely emotional disturbed kids who had been neglected and abused. It was a good job, but it didn't pay much and it was too far away with my dad being at home with us. I told friends, "Now that I have a house I need a good paying, local job."

I had faith and almost like a miracle, I was soon hired by the local University hospital as a medical social worker for their home care division, making $8,000 more per year than my other job. I was 55, and was finally making money above the poverty level. A true success story. Social workers, without an MSW, are not the most respected positions when it comes to salaries.

After we were in the house for a couple of months my 28 year-old son came to live with us. He used my daughter Rebecca's bedroom during the week and slept on the couch on weekends when she came to stay with her brother's and me. Two months later, with the garage renovated, I made plans to go down and get dad. I told my mother that when I come get him, she would come up with me and visit for a week and see what I had set up. She appreciated that. I wanted her to know things would be safe and okay for dad. It wasn't an impressive set-up, but it was home and I knew it was going to work.

Almost as if an omen, the week before I was to pick him up, I received an 11:00 p.m. phone call from my mother: She was nervous and upset, "The Care Home called and told me they can't find dad. They say he's been gone since 7:00. They just called me now and said they called the police." She wanted to know if she should go there and help.

"No mom," I was emphatic, "just stay at home, you can't do anything; they'll find him. Don't worry." Don't worry? What else could I tell her? I called The Care Home and was told they were looking. They had no idea where he was after supper. Nothing surprises me when it comes to care in any facility that does this work. In Gainesville one nursing home lost a resident for five days until she was found dead in a closet right next to the nurses station. I was praying dad would be found soon without any problems.

My mother called a few times to check in and get some support. I kept reassuring her he would be fine. Who really knew? The ACLF was located near a main street in Ft. Lauderdale with as many crazies as any place. Finally, at 2:00 a.m. mom called to tell me they found him across the street sitting in a Laundromat. He was okay. I told mom I'd bring them both to Gainesville in two days.

CHAPTER 4

Dad Moves To Gainesville

I left with Rebecca, my mission companion, to bring my parents to Gainesville. We picked up my mom and went to visit dad to pack his things for the following day when we would return to Gainesville. Arriving at the ACLF we found my dad standing alone in the middle of the day room with his pants soaking wet from urine. He seemed a little spaced out. One of the aides came up to us and put her arm around him saying how much she was going to miss him. A couple of other women, also came up and said about the same thing, showing a lot of sincere caring for him, but none of them suggested changing his pants. Odd? Typical? Who knows why none of them took him and cleaned him up? Was it like this every day? Well, it was his last day, so when my mother wanted to complain to the management, I didn't want us to get into it then. It was late and I persuaded my mom that we take him up to his room and get him cleaned up and ready for bed.

When I opened the door to his room there was a women standing there. I assumed she was either the woman he held hands with, or another resident who was lost.

The women told me this wasn't my dad's room anymore. I told her he wasn't leaving until tomorrow. My mother stood there, dumbfounded and couldn't imagine what was going on. The lady began to explain to us that dad had wet his bed the night before and they moved him to another room. I asked her a few times what she was doing there, and she, who was a bit confused also, finally told us she was a private nurse caring for the new man in the room.

Talk about confusing.

We finally convinced this woman that my dad was staying in the room one more night. The four of us, Dad, Mom, Becca and me were still standing in the doorway talking to this woman, when she finally left and we went in the room to get dad settled for his last night. Dad's bed was unmade, no sheet, no blanket. My mom assumed that they were getting rid of him before he was intended to leave. The private nurse told us she thought they may have gotten busy and forgot to make his bed, since the sheets and blanket were on the night table. I agreed with her;

found an attendant who I asked to shower him since he was urine soaked, as Mom and I made the bed.

The following day we loaded some of dad's clothes from the condo, went to the Concord and gathered up his sparse belongings and off we went on a new and different adventure. For what it was worth I did mention to the management about no one changing him when they saw he was wet, and I received their lame apologies. Typical!

As we drove the 6 hours home I had a thousand thoughts about what was going on. Although I was working on this for two years, the thought of 'what am I doing?' roamed off and on through my head. A single, working parent taking his senile father to live with him and his four kids. It was nothing I ever heard of anyone doing. I have been unique through most of my life and thought of how 23 years earlier I began caring for my now 28 year-old son when his mother was no longer able to care of him due to her alcoholism and mental instability. I followed my intuition with my son, and now I was following that same inner guide. A feeling of specialness swelled in me, not pride, but the realization that something deep in me sees what is in front of me and deals with it as best as I can. There was also a trust of what appears sweet and holy in life. Deep inside of me, this new circumstance fit that description.

Yes, it was terribly confusing for me to have three young children in my home and bring in my father. We all did the best we could. I don't know, decades later, whether there was unresolved trauma to any of my children. Since the publisher of this book is requiring me to get permission from all those whose names are used in this book, I will also request of my children, if they choose, to write their own assessment of those two years we cared for my father in our home.

CHAPTER 5

The Plan

The plan was for my 16 year-old son Jacob to begin most of the caregiving while I was at work. Jacob quit school a year earlier in order to do self-study, and recently was the youngest student accepted at the local Massage School in Gainesville. He'd be able to stay with his grandfather for the first three months before beginning school. I paid him $100 a week from the $700 a month I was getting from my dad's social security check so Jacob could save that money for his first installment on his school tuition. When he started school I'd need another plan. Miguel, my 28 year old, was looking for work so he helped Jacob until he found a job. It was a good plan. There was a slight uneasiness about what was going on, but overall I had confidence things were going to work out.

If dad had medical problems I would have been a bit more leery about taking this on, but at 82 he had never been in the hospital, no diabetes, no heart problem, his lungs were all right, no medications, except for a diuretic for edema in his feet and a stool softener.

I stopped the diuretic right away and began giving him a banana each morning to help with his potassium level which hopefully would help reduce his edema.

That first week my mom shared a bedroom with dad. She continued relating to him with the same confrontational patterns that had been part of their life for years, expecting him to do what she wanted and how she wanted him to do it. It's a pattern that they both bought into and neither is to blame. His resignation to how things were, used to bother me, but now that he couldn't do much for himself, it was something that I just had to accept, but also felt his protector and advocate, especially against my mother's irrational, domineering will. I had apprehensions about how we would get along that week, because of her impatience and rigidity, but actually the week didn't go too badly with so many in a small house. I suppose there was some flexibility on all our parts in making this first week with dad work out so the tension levels did not get too high. Mom as it turned out, was actually considerate in how she talked with the kids, although I had to remind her a few times to lay off my father when he wasn't responding as a normal minded person. She didn't want to, or wasn't able to understand, or was it denial, in regard to what was going on with him and his limitations. She was around him for his year at the Concord; she should have known, but instead, intractable would best describe how she interacted with him.

Into our second month the day-to-day routine worked out so dad was not too confused by being there with us, on the other hand he was totally confused about what was going on.

For the first couple of weeks he wanted to know when he was going home. When I'd ask him where home was, he said "Around the corner." Jacob, in trying to accommodate his grandfather went along with his grandfather wanting to go home. Jacob allowed grandpa to "straighten things up" around the house before he left to "go home." They went out the front door, walked around the side of the house turned around and back in the front door, and grandpa said, "Here we are back home." Jacob did this with him three or four times, since dad always wanted to "go home," then felt he was back there. At some point, after a few days, he no longer wanted to go back home, maybe feeling he had arrived.

His memory for the most part is gone. Short term, long term and most of in between. He remembers his name, who I am, although he calls me "pop." He couldn't remember the names of my kids, or where he's living, or where he lived for 20 years with my mom in Ft. Lauderdale. When friends of mine asked him where he had been living, sometimes he couldn't remember anything, and sometimes he said New Jersey, where he hadn't lived for over 40 years. No matter how much he was reminded, it was gone moments later. All typical of fourth stage Alzheimer's patients.

Even the one year living in the Concord, where he just left a few weeks ago, nothing, like a blur, if that, except he was able to recall the women he was holding hands with, although not her name, which he probably never knew.

Because he was an avid walker for years to keep him limber, we regularly took him for walks in the neighborhood. His gait was fair at times and then he would begin to slow down and shuffle his feetn barely lifting them off the ground. We had to keep reminding him to move his feet and then he'd resume lifting them for a few yards and then back to the shuffle. He also leaned forward as he walked giving the impression he was going to fall forward. He told Jacob he did that when he was going uphill, even though the ground was always level. His balance was way off, so when he stood, sometimes he'd rock backward, or if he turned around he sometimes was not able to without tipping a bit. Some of this was more pronounced when we went for walks in markets or department stores, where there were large groups of people. Walking then was even more difficult, coming to a complete stop and staggering, almost slumping to the floor. In the lobby of a movie theater I felt afraid he was going to go down and kept asking him if he was okay. He's a hard one to judge because he never says there's a problem. I asked him if he was collapsing and he said he wasn't going to collapse, but "I might fall down." He did regain his awareness of what to do and made it to his seat, with difficulty, in the darkened theater.

I took dad for a general check up at the hospital where I worked as a social worker. I wanted information about the hernia protruding in his groin. The doctor that examined him didn't feel it should be operated on, but told me that a truss should help take care of the problem. They did find a bit of blood in his stools and the doctor, who I worked with, suggested a sigmoidoscopy, which is where they take a tube with a viewer and insert it up the large intestine a foot or so. Because I felt pressure to take care of dad so that I wouldn't be criticized by my sister and mother, I made the appointment for the procedure... although I had my reluctance.

The morning prior to the procedure he had to drink a small bottle of a laxative, than I gave him an enema. That cleaned him out some, but I knew he wasn't totally cleaned out, because he wasn't having

bowel movements regularly. When they began the
procedure they found his intestines were still too
blocked to see if he had polyps or anything else
growing up there, so they gave him another enema.

Because he hadn't been drinking liquids regularly,
the enemas apparently caused him to become quickly
dehydrated. His blood pressure dropped quickly, he
turned white and came very close to passing out. I
sensed he wasn't doing well at all, but wasn't sure how
worried I should be until I saw the doctor and nurses,
who I knew, becoming alarmed. They began taking
his blood pressure every few minutes, and when they
hooked him up to IV of water I realized they were
worried about what was happening to him. Then
slowly after about 15 minutes on the IV his color
returned and he was more conscious.

Because he was prepped and ready the doctor
suggested we take him to the area of the hospital
where they could monitor him better to see if they
could continue with what had begun. I helped move
him on a gurney up to the 7th floor of the hospital.
When we were there they made all their preparations
to do the peeping into his intestine, only to find he
still had a huge, dark colored, piece of feces, which
would leave his sigmoid area too cloudy, or too dark
to see anything clearly. They decided to make another
appointment in two weeks. I took him home and he

immediately went to sleep for three hours, waking up feeling good.

Although I work in a hospital I generally don't like them much, or a lot of what they do. That pretty much applies to the whole allopathic medical industry. For the past 20 years I've used, almost exclusively, alternative methods of healing, including homeopathy, acupuncture, massage therapy, herbal and mind over matter healing. I believe it works, have seen it work and although western medicine may be needed at times, the other, less intrusive methods are more to my liking. I was blessed never having to use allopathic medicine for my children or myself, so to take my father in for that exam was something out of my previous experience. I felt there wasn't any negative feelings about what we were doing, but in being honest with myself we did need to know if he had anything wrong with his intestine. My gut, funny, my gut and his gut, feeling, though, was that the blood in his stools was from him straining from not having regular bowel movements and he wasn't drinking enough daily liquids.

He remembered what happened to him at the hospital and when I told him they wanted him to go back he said, "Not on me." I felt the same way. One of the nurses, who helped him during his minor crisis, gave me a bundle of cards to smear feces on to check for blood. She also gave me the liquid to put on it so

I didn't have to send it in to be checked. That is how I dealt with the problem, and my testing proved there was no excessive blood.

One of dad's wonderful qualities is that he was an easy going, kind and gentle man and was easy to get along with. Occasionally he would verbally jump on the kids for doing something he didn't approve of, but if I told him it was no big deal, "Dad they are not hurting anything," he would let go of his idea, and said, "If its okay with you, it's okay with me."

He's also a good, non-complaining eater. And since we had a vegetarian household it made things easy that he was not insisting on animal food. He never complained about what we had to eat, usually finishing everything on his plate. He hadn't been much of a meat eater the past few years, but when he was at the ACLF I knew they had meat of one sort or another, for almost all the meals. I was slightly concerned about the transition, but he was getting all the nutrients he needed so he wasn't suffering any negative effects with our hardy diet.

One day I took dad for a walk around the neighborhood. The kids had done this in the past as I had, but that day he wasn't able to complete the few blocks without getting very weak and not being able to continue. I reminded him to move his feet, which he did for a few steps, but then again he slowed and I had to hold him up. He kept leaning forward, saying he has to do this when he's going up hill. There were no hills. All very flat sidewalks. I tried to see if stopping to rest would give him the energy to continue, but after a while realized he couldn't go on. Becca was with us so I sent her to get Miguel with the car.

A few days later we couldn't find grandpa for a short while. Gabe had never taken him for a walk, but had told his friend who was at the house that he was taking grandpa out. I became concerned about Gabe going too far and grandpa not being able to walk home. So I began driving the neighborhood and Jacob biked around looking for them. I finally found them down the street about three blocks. They had walked to the traffic light about five blocks away. When I pulled up to them he was in okay shape, walking very slowly, laughing that, "It was not really any kind of walk." Maybe he was even recalling that he used to walk for miles. He had no problem making it back to the house with no assistance.

I took grandpa for another short two block walk two days later but again he was barely able to make it. That was early in the day, Gabe's walk with him two days previously was late in the day. When I've gone shopping with him and he struggled with keeping balance and continuing to walk, it was late in the day. I was hoping this morning he wouldn't have any trouble with such walk, but for whatever the reason he asked to stop, but didn't, until I took his arm and told him to slow down and rest a bit. We had to do that two or three times in a short distance. When we got home he laid down on the chaise lounge outside and rested.

I found it hard to get a grip on his limits because they seemed to keep changing. One day he walked well then he couldn't go as far. One day he put his clothes on or off easily, the next day he needed help. One day there's confusion about where he was and the next day he seemed comfortable. We had to keep adjusting to his differences, which was okay, since we are the caregivers.

One problem common with many Alzheimer's people is their frustration and anger. Because he is such a mellow person we didn't experience this to any great degree, except on occasions.

One night I was helping him get ready for bed, and he became very angry. It was only a brief moment, but he yelled at me, "Why is everyone always telling me what to do?" And he threw his pajama top. I felt he wanted to express more anger, but I spoke to him with soft kind words and told him we're only trying to help him. I expected him to tell me he didn't need any help, but he calmly allowed me to help him get ready for bed.

There was also one night when he began to yell at Jacob and some of his friends who were down in the boy's room. Yelling "What are you doing there? Who are you? Keep the noise down or I'll have to throw you out?" It was odd, but there was something in his tone, or the words, that reminded me of when I was a kid when he yelled at me and my friends for something. Fortunately this didn't happen much when I was a kid.

One evening when I came home from visiting friends he was in an angry mood. Miguel said he had a hard time with him for the past couple of hours, grandpa complaining and raising his voice in irritation over something, in part confusion about who lived here, and being confused about kids, his mother, his father, my own mother. When I asked him about my mother, his wife, he wanted to know if she knew he was there and where she was and when was she going to be here. I hoped if he talked with her on the phone he would become a bit more oriented to person, so I called her.

Before I put my dad on, I had to listen to her berate me about her hurt feelings because I forgot her birthday that week. As if I had nothing to do. She was good at laying guilt trips on me. After listening and listening, and me being very apologetic, I gave the phone to dad. He was still confused and had no idea who he was talking to. He kept referring to her as "mamma," and was actually uncomfortable, or unable to express anything to her. When she told him she was his wife and that his mother and father were dead, he handed me the phone angry for her telling him that his parents were dead. He also told her we weren't feeding him, but that I was feeding my kids, and he didn't live here with me, or with anyone else. "I don't live anyplace, I live out in the street," is what he said. He was almost 100% without any memory of anything, but I felt when he told her that we weren't feeding him he was enjoying giving her impression that we didn't take care of him. It was only a glance, but when I said, "Oh, come on dad, we feed you," he just looked up at me continuing to tell her either an intentional fabrication, or since he wasn't remembering, he may have not known he was getting fed anyplace.

I finally asked for the phone and explained to mom, who was feeling extremely distressed from the talk, which was the worst incident of forgetfulness we had experienced with him and hopefully it wouldn't last. He actually hadn't been hard to deal with when these incidents happened, and was only difficult when he was totally out of touch as he was that evening. Although he was never this type of person, I told the boys that we had to be aware of any tendency he might have of to get violent. I told the kids not to antagonize him when he was being that way, but to try and be as gentle and clear to him about what was going on which may or may not bring him back to here and now.

About 10 minutes after the talk with my mom she called back to tell me not to come get her the following week for Thanksgiving. She may have been blown away by dad's total confusion. She said she'd take a bus or train up to see us in a couple of weeks. I really didn't think it was a good idea, but I wasn't enthused about driving down to get her one day and coming back the next. She finally said that we were all younger so why don't we come down there. I told her we weren't all able to come. She then changed it around that maybe I could come get her in a couple of weeks when we had more time to plan it. I wouldn't have to drive back the next day, but give myself a day of visiting and then return. The fact that she was going back and forth with the plans were an indication some confusion was going on with her, but I told her that sounded like a better idea. We would wait until Christmas. Then she asked to speak to dad again.

I gave the phone back to him, telling him again, it was Mae, his wife. This time he was perfectly clear about where he was and that everything was all right. They spoke for about two or three minutes, but it was as if he had come back from someplace and was a different person. We all noticed it sitting around him in the living room listening to him talk, even

Becca, who was 12, commented about how he had "Come back."

DAD'S STAND UP COMEDY ROUTINE

I'm not sure if he's dreaming at night, or what, but he's come up with some funny lines when I wake and see him going towards the bathroom.

"Where you going dad," I asked one night as he was walking out of his room? You going to pee?"

"No."

"Where you going then?"

"To see Kulick."

"Whose Kulick?"

"The furrier."

"What's a furrier, I asked him?"

"He sells furs. Uncle Sam (he used to have an uncle Sam) told me to go see Kulick."

That was it. Then he went to pee and back to bed.

The next day I told him about "Kulick the furrier," and he had a good laugh about Kulick.

On another night when he was up to the bathroom, he told me he was going to make two movies. One was about "Joe the Schmoe," and the other about "Jake the Snake." He and I had a good laugh about those two lines after he went to the bathroom and I was tucking him into bed. Actually there was some basis for those two characters. In the bathroom, I have a great picture of the three stooges standing with golf clubs and their typical dumb expression on their faces. Dad gave his own names to them then he and Jacob talked about them for a week. Dad made up funny names for them with both he and Jacob laughing heartily. Some evenings we all joked about the picture and the names he had given them.

December 18,, 1993

A woman I know gave my phone number to a lady named Eleanor who called one night to talk with me about helping care for my father. During our conversation it dawned on me that I had met Eleanor at an outdoor festival. At the time I was actually interested in knowing her better and called her but she said she was going away for a few months and wasn't interested in adding anyone or anything else to her life. But here she was returning. I wondered how life works.

Two days later Eleanor came to our house where we had a good talk about her helping take care of dad. She was seriously interested. She sort of chattered on and on about a variety of things, but she had experience caring for the elderly, was a massage therapist and was involved in spiritual pursuits. She's also in the midst of a water fast and doing daily colonics, and is a vegetarian, and into sound health.

Seemed too good to be true. She couldn't begin until after Xmas and then she could only help for a few months because in April she was going to the Abode of the Message, a Sufi spiritual community, in upstate New York.

December 20, 1993

I talked with Eleanor a couple of times and she seemed to be just right. She came over one night to get to know dad and my household better and very kindly invited me to her house the next night for a massage. Naturally, I accepted.

Next night

Eleanor gave me a wonderful, thorough massage, by the fireplace in her living room. After that, I'm not sure how it happened, but she was gave me a little kiss, that I made into a more than friendly bigger one, and I ended up spending the night with her. My first night of making love to anyone in five years. This was real and enjoyable and I thought I liked her a lot, but didn't feel real in love. One night. We'll see what we will see. It was a welcome Christmas gift from the divine.

CHRISTMAS

Being from a Jewish background we really didn't celebrate Christmas, but I did bring my mother up to visit for a few days and it was not good. Holidays, joyousness, for many families, not for us. Too bad. She was difficult for us to deal with, continuing to insist that she was right about everything. This was especially true in how she was dealing with dad; always insisting that she knew what was best for him, when she had no clue about his difficulties. I was taking her home the next day and it was a relief to the family.

The next day I went by to see Eleanor before taking my mother home. Eleanor and I were unsure how to act to each other, but were nice and comfortable sharing some hugs and gentle kisses. I left as she was off on a few days meditation retreat. Interesting meeting someone to care for my father and she is into many of the things in life that I am.

When Eleanor returned from her retreat we continued seeing each other, me going to her house after dad was put to bed and she staying at my house sometimes. My kids being on the alert for him during the night when I was at her house. Then, she began to stay at my house more often and at some point I suggested she move in with us since she was there much of the time. Although she had a very large house, we had fallen in love and this seemed like a natural step since she was at my house every day anyway. It was a very difficult step for her, since she had been living alone, and now, a houseful of people, in such a small house. It had it's strain on her, as well as on Miguel, who had a hard time with her nature of wanting to help so much, do so much and even wanting to help him with his drinking and smoking. I had to ask him to respect who she was to me, and not get into any arguments with her. Fortunately, or unfortunately, there were only a few weeks of her being with us before she went on a spiritual retreat.

February 4,, 1994

It's been almost two months since my last entry. There's been no improvement or decline in dad's condition. There was a week in particular when he had loose uncontrolled bowel movements needing cleaned at least once a day, sometimes a few times a day. It was especially difficult for Eleanor because she had to change him a number of times during the day, but I also had my fill of helping him out of his clothes into the shower, my preferred way of handling those messes.

I didn't like having the thought, but I wondered whether I was already getting burnt out on the care of my dad. It crossed my mind whether I should be looking for a place to put him or to have him on some meds so he sleeps through the night and not wake me. I looked at myself, realizing it had only been a few months that he's been with us. It made me feel like I was faltering in my task. Two things were especially bothering me: his diarrhea, and him getting up so much at night. His diarrhea stopped with the help of a drugstore anti-diarrhea pill and his sleeping pattern, although he was still getting up during the night, it wasn't three times a night and if it was I'm wasn't aware of each time. Eleanor was spending some of her nights with me and she was considerable help in getting up with him, but I felt it is my work, my dad, so I tried to do it, but she was so insistent. That made it easy for me to just turn over and go back to sleep making it easier for me to get up in the morning to go to work.

One night when I heard him making noise in his bedroom I got up. It was 3:00 a.m. and he was dressed. "Where ya goin dad," I asked. He said he didn't know, so I waited with him as he got undressed and went back to bed. I put a sign up in the bathroom above the sink that says, "Dad, I love you, Don't get dressed until the sun comes up. Your son, Robert." I told him I was making the sign. He said it was a good idea. I first put another sign on the bed opposite his and shut the lights, then realized he couldn't read it in the dark. We both laughed at that one. So the bathroom was the next best place to remind him not to get dressed in the middle of the night.

DAD GETS LOST

Dad was lost in the neighborhood on two occasions going out the door before any one knew he was gone. The first time was soon after I left for work in the morning. Eleanor called to tell me she was busy around the house not paying attention to him since it was still early with him usually in bed until 10:00 and boom he was gone. I told Eleanor to begin looking for him and I would call 911. When I called 911, the emergency operator asked my dad's name and she said she thought they had picked up an Ellenberg. She checked and told me they did have him and were bringing him back home. He must have given them his last name. The operator said they had received calls from neighbors who were reporting him walking around the neighborhood. Eleanor called to tell me the police brought him home in his underpants with a tennis racket in one hand and his truss in the other. No wonder people were calling.

Quite a picture; enough for a laugh and not a worry. In fact I didn't panic at all knowing he would be found. There was the possibility of him walking into traffic, or into someone's yard, falling or something happening and not being found. This is another problem for people with AD, they sometimes have to be literally locked into a house, or eventually can't be at home with family, but in a secure setting.

The second time he walked off, for some reason it made me more afraid for his safety since I was more aware anything could happen to him to walking aimlessly in our neighborhood. All we did was turn our backs for ten minutes and he was gone. Nur Allah, Eleanor's spiritual name, was giving me a massage on the back porch with dad right there and then he went inside the house. Nur Allah went into the house for a phone call, and when she was off the phone he was gone. We looked up and down the street and didn't see him. He had disappeared so quickly. I called 911 and a police car came out. I gave them a description and we all went around the neighborhood. Nur Allah was gone the longest, while Becca and I stayed out on the sidewalk near the house discussing what could happen, sort of expecting, hoping, he would just come walking down the street. Soon a neighbor yells to us from across the street that, "She found him a few blocks away." In a short while Nur Allah came home with him saying how she got lost herself. Dad felt no worse for being lost and said causally it, "Wasn't the first time." I tried to have him understand that it wasn't just for fun and things could happen to him like being lost in the woods or falling and not being found. I got frustrated. What was the use? He stood listening , only partially paying attention because it didn't make any difference to him being alive wasn't a this or that and he felt no pain from his ordeal. Maybe my explanation sunk in because he never walked off again, even though after a while we was spending time outside in the backyard without us watching over him.

Actually him getting lost that second time could have been serious: Nur Allah was led to him by a kid on a bike. The kid excitedly told her he knew where dad was and took Nur Allah to a wooded area where she found him hanging on to a sapling. It was about a quarter mile from the house. How did he get so far so quickly when sometimes he was unable to walk one block? Maybe some one has an explanation for that; I've no clue.

Feb. 28, 1994

I took Dad and Becca to Ft. Lauderdale to see my mom while my sister and her daughter, 17 year-old Carly, were visiting also. It could have been a wonderful time, but instead it was an emotional, family disaster, mostly because of how my mother was and how we all ended up relating to her. Tina, in recent years was having a more difficult time being around our mother and stayed in a hotel rather then spend her nights at our mother's condo. It would have been tight, one bedroom, couches, floor, Becca and I could deal, but for Tina it was worth the piece of mind to not deal with mother with all of us so compactly in her apartment. With Tina's husband slowly getting sicker and sicker from cancer she needed the rest from our mother's constant criticism, nagging, complaining, and unhappy, unsmiling countenance. What a drag for me to have to express those attitudes of my mother. But it is who she is!

It was distressing. I felt bothered that we just weren't getting along. From each of us to her, there was disrespect. I became so irritated at her at one point I told her she was, "fucked up." I later apologized, to my 80 year-old mother. But it was out and I was very bothered at myself for allowing those words to come out. But every little thing became an issue to her until there were no other words to say to her to get the point across.

As usual she wasn't very nice to dad. She didn't have any more patience than she ever had for his difficult times. No real reason why she should. At 80 years she wasn't going to change her habits and patterns; especially with her husband, regardless of his mental condition. When it came time for him to get to sleep the first night she insisted that he sleep on a narrow fold out chair she had in her bedroom. She was mostly afraid that he would urinate and wet the living room fold out couch, even though there were plastic sheets we could use. I was a bit taken aback that she was so adamant about it and even when I suggested that he sleep on the couch with me, she turned it around, with no logic, and said she would sleep on the couch and we should sleep in her bed. I finally convinced her it made more sense for us to be in the living room and that she remain in her bed. She covered the mattress with two plastic sheets to make sure no urine got on the mattress otherwise she "would have to sell the couch." She also insisted that when we used the bathroom at night we wouldn't go through her room.

That night I woke up hearing her use the bathroom and when she was back in bed I woke dad for him to use it. Before I could direct him into the hall to the bathroom, he went through her bedroom. She yelled out, complaining we were keeping her awake. I said, "You're awake anyway," and she said, "that it didn't make any difference."

That's her nature. I understood she was 80 years old, and maybe couldn't think clearly, but what was going on were patterns of behavior that had been long entrenched in her mind. Mainly, it was her inflexible nature, defending what she thought was right, even as she was the only one seeing something that way.

Dad became angry with her a number of times for bothering him, over what were small issues. The first night she was pulling on his shirt while he was taking it off. She wouldn't let go. He finally grabbed it off and threw it on the floor, kicking it across the floor away from her. It was one thing after another, but it's been that way for years and I had the feeling he had his fill of her being a controller over his life. He yelled at her like he sometimes did when he was angry with my sons. Now, with my mother, there were more things to annoy him than at home, although at home there were things to annoy him but we didn't seem to bother him that much and sometimes they did. Like the door slamming when the kids go in or out. It's odd to see this quiet sensitive man lose control and lash out at anyone. I had the feeling he, like many, kept a lot of anger towards others, in this case, his wife, repressed inside.

When we arrived at their condo he was happy to see her, when we left he seemed to feel a bit of a loss and briefly confused that we were leaving, but other than that he showed no real feeling connection towards her. Because of her lack of sensitivity it was probably easy for him to forget who she is, although forgetting loved ones, is common with Alzheimer's patients in general.

On the other hand he has the sensitivity of a saint. While we were visiting my mother, Becca's mother called to tell me that Becca's pet cat had died suddenly and she didn't want us to get home too late so we could have a burial service. She didn't want me to tell Becca to save her from being upset during our visit that wasn't so pleasant anyway. When we arrived back in Gainesville, Linda, Becca's mom, told Becca about her cat and my broken hearted daughter, went through a lot of crying; we held her allowing her the discharge of emotion. After a while we took the cat, laid it out on some blankets, and into a hole that had previously been dug. Dad walked out there with us into the wooded area. When he saw Becca very tearful he also became emotional and took Becca in his arms and held her. He did this a couple of times in the next 15 minutes and she easily went into his arms. He actually told her "it's okay to cry and let it out." I felt this was the most tender experience I had ever seen; my 83 year-old father with dementia, comforting my 13 year-old daughter, crying in each other arms. He showed such compassion and sense of feeling for Becca; the moment itself, etched forever in my memory. I felt here was the saintliness that I have recognized in him before; in that moment, so obvious. It's sad for me to say, but I couldn't help contrast that with the time we just spent with his wife of over 50 years who couldn't feel that kind of compassion for anyone.

That is something I don't want to believe of my own mother, but the truth is that she does not feel for others. Her children, yes, but still unable to give a lot of feeling from deep within herself. I've tried to give her some feeling from me. I really believe that a deep part of me was attempting to give to her something she may have never had just to help her feel a bit happier. She rejects that in me as in others. She lives on the surface of life and never, maybe from fear, wanted to explore depths of feeling within, blaming her parents for their lack of affection to her.

I felt sad about the unfortunate state of our family when children and parents can't be around each other for very long. It is really sad about us, all so different, but I feel bad because families need to be harmonious and compassionate in times of need. I don't want to blame my mother for her feelings, she just didn't know how she was growing old with disinterest in her own feelings, or missing something about having feelings for life and humanity. There is also her inability to agree with another person; adamantly, maybe desperately holding onto any idea she has had, even if no one agrees with her. It is strong will, but based more on fear. Fear, of loosing who she is; holding onto concepts that protect her vulnerable inner child. Total none acceptance of another person's point of view. Through all this I was understanding more and more about our dysfunctional family.

March 21, 1994

I finally arranged for dad to go to the Alzheimer's Day Program. He seems to be enjoying it. I set it up after Eleanor kept prodding me to get things together so when she leaves to go on retreat at the Abode of the Message, I would still have things covered. Maybe I wait longer then others in getting things together, but always seem to get things worked out. Miguel will be at home part time and Gabe once in a while. Gabe was with him a few nights ago when I went out. Dad became belligerent with Gabe and angry and told him and his friend Sequoia to go downstairs. He was loud and I guess threatening. Gabe was able to call Jacob who was at a friends house. Grandpa was usually even tempered with Jacob, but remained hostile until Jacob convinced grandpa that he was his grandson and who each was. Then he went to bed. I reminded the boys again, that we have to watch out that in his irrational anger, he doesn't strike out. He has never done anything like that in his life that I know of, so in some respects it is inconceivable, on the other hand that does occurs to some AD people.

Gabe, at 14, was now understandably feeling reluctant to be alone with grandpa, and wasn't feeling so sure before this latest incident. I think it can work for a short time, but Gabe was right suggesting I wear my beeper when I go out.

Miguel took grandpa for a nice walk today around the neighborhood. Miguel sounded good letting me know what they had done.

August 15, 1994

Dad has begun to be more and more incontinent, peeing almost every night in his bed and a few times during the day. I was putting diapers on him regularly wondering if he's now peeing more easily in bed and in his pants because of the diapers. Does he know the difference? I doubt it. I also began putting down the absorbent pads under a draw sheet on his bed because the urine is going through diaper, sheet and pad, with the bottom sheet usually remaining dry.

We're going into a new stage soon with Miguel going to work in two weeks. Jacob has agreed to stay with grandpa during the day for a while until I can get someone else. Again, I have to go on faith that someone will appear who we need. It is only three full days, since two days he goes to the Als Place, so they only have to get him ready in the morning and be at home in the afternoon when he returns from the Alzheimer's program.

He still finds Gabe as someone to yell at, sometimes with no provocation, or none that has any significance except to him. Yelling loudly if Gabe's pants are down too low and he has to keep pulling them up, which annoys me, but I was thinking of stages a 14 year-old goes through. Or Gabe might be laughing at something that dad doesn't understand, or if Gabe just passes through the room without saying hello. I asked Gabe to try and be more friendly. Ask Grandpa, "How you doing, how was your day, say hello, relate a bit more personally. Come on Gabe I know it isn't fun sometimes but give it a try." Gabe agreed and today came in and did all what we discussed the other day. I think he knows how he has been and maybe will make some changes in how he will relate to his grandfather.

Gabe had put out some kind energy initially with grandpa, but got thrown off by grandpa's irritation towards him. These were incidents that annoyed Gabe, like the time grandpa wanted to go see the Pope and Gabe was the only one at home. Grandpa got dressed, which he would do some mornings, and walked out the door. Gabe went after him, asking him where he was going, "To see the Pope." Gabe told me later, he asked grandpa, "Why do you want to see the pope?" "I have to tell him something." Gabe tried to reason with him, but to no avail, so they ended up walking a few blocks until grandpa couldn't walk any more, and began to slump to the ground. Fortunately, some one stopped and helped grandpa into the car, unfortunately, that car ran out of gas in three blocks back to the house, so they got out but by then, grandpa was able to continue. The whole incident really upset Gabe, although he hung in and did what he had to do. I'm not sure how I would have reacted if I was that 14 year-old.

Dad and I were home alone one evening when I began doing some writing in my room. He walked back there and asked, "Can I lie down?" It was a nice feeling, warm, homelike, with him there as I try and be creative. He scooted and pulled himself up to my pillow after sitting on the corner of the bed, almost half on and half off. That's another one of his idiosyncrasies, not setting full butt on a chair. Almost all the time when he goes to sit down he catches himself, half on and half off, also, sitting, sometimes a foot away from the table. There was the whole bed, box spring with a futon on top right on the floor; he walked into the room and with the whole bed in front of him, sat right on the corner that was closest to him as he approached the bed. Maybe something in him didn't want to go any further so he plotzes where he sees a place. This idea was just coming to me as I wrote. I wondered if his poor judgment in sitting down was a function of poor sight. He seems to see well in the distance and can read signs in the street and what is on TV, but up close he isn't good at all and can only read headlines in the newspapers. I asked him if he wanted magazines in large print but he said no. I will make sure I bring or get him some magazines with large print anyway. He never was much of a reader and with his memory gone, I'm not sure what he could understand.

I was working on an article with dad on the bed when suddenly my friend Tom is at the bedroom door. Tom comes in my room and says hello to Jerry. I tell Dad, Tom and I were going to talk in the kitchen and he can keep resting in my bed. Tom and I were in the kitchen a short while when dad came out to tell us he was going home. I remind him again he was home and he looked at me like I was making up a story. "No dad," I tell him, "We live here. Me, you, my son's." Basically the same story I tell him all the time when he spaces out completely and has no idea what's going on.

After Tom left Dad and I sat on the couch talking about him and how he can't remember things. I let him know that we love him and like him living with us. Then again, he asks me about Mae, and if she knew where he was. I patiently go over the past year and a half, oh, maybe it's two years already and tell him again "Dad you haven't been living with Mae but she is at home and now you are here. She doesn't want to come live here, but she visits and we visit her." He asks me, "Does she like it here when she visits? "Not so much, that's why she isn't living here, but maybe she will change her mind." That evening we had a very warm close feeling. He seemed to feel that too, but for him it's gone, for me, it'll last awhile, especially, doing this journaling.

After we talked for 15 minutes he asked me, "Does Tina know I'm here?" Ah, good, remembering his daughter. "Yeah," I tell him, "Tina knows you're here," reminding him we saw her in Ft. Lauderdale a few weeks ago, "She was there with her daughter Carley. You and I were there with Rebecca, your two granddaughters." He liked being reminded that he had two granddaughters. He accepted my explanation of what is going on and seemed comfortable. I told him I was going to call Tina because I hadn't talked with her in two weeks, since she told me she had pneumonia. Life is so difficult for her at this time that I'm not sure how much she wants to talk with me about it because of the pain.

When all that strain comes on someone they are not breathing well and some people get pneumonia or other lung problems.

I called her and she said her pneumonia had just gotten better and she was back to work and her husband had taken my advice and gone down to the Hypocratic Institute in West Palm Beach to learn more about natural healing through food, about himself, his inner and outer being.

It was only a quarter to 10:00 and dad wanted to go to bed. usual, he usually wants to stay up until 11:00, 11:30 and resisted when we asked him to go to bed earlier. I guided him to the bathroom to pee, take his teeth out and into the bedroom that he recalled it looking familiar. Taking off his clothes sitting on the opposite bed tonight asking where he should put his pants. He threw them onto his sleeping bed, and I let him know he switched sides and straightened him out. When he got in bed he didn't lay on his back, but laid on his side sort of fetal-like, but not real tight, with his knees. He seemed to feel or looked almost childlike, as if he had done something wrong or something was going on that he didn't understand which he doesn't. It felt like he wanted to be in bed because he didn't know how to deal with what was happening to him. Like something is wrong and he can't fix it, and being in bed is one way of not having to contend.

I know I was reading into what he was doing, but something seemed different in his feeling. When I said goodnight to him and shut his light he said good night to me with a, "God Bless" which he never said before. So, maybe my perception of what he was feeling was close to right.

MARCH 1995

Eleanor left again for another Sufi retreat weekend, this one in Atlanta. In a short time she will be leaving for a year. When dad got up I took care of his morning, getting him dressed and fed. After I left for work he told the boys he was going to a movie on Westchester Avenue, which must have been in the Bronx or a dream or the Bronx and a dream. Jacob and Ariel went with him for a few blocks until they were able to persuade him to come home. Gabe beeped me and told me what was going on. I called back later and talked with dad and told him there no movie theatres in the neighborhood trying to convince him we weren't anyplace near Westchester Ave and he would have to walk a 1000 miles to get there. He listened to me for about five minutes, seemed to understand but kept asking me where the movie was. I told him a few times to have breakfast with raisins and bananas and some juice. He repeated he was going to the movie, again I reminded him about his grandson's and that Jacob was not feeling well and maybe he could help him feel better. While on the phone he asked Gabe, "Howyou feeling?" Thinking it was Jacob. Finally he seemed to be in the present moment enough for me to hang up and the rest of the day went okay for him.

That evening he peed his pants while eating supper and I changed him. While sitting watching TV that evening I thought I was smelling b.m. but didn't mention it, instead decided give him a shower since he was going to the Als Place in the morning. Yes, I did find b.m. in his underpants. While sitting on the potty chair, that I use for a shower chair, he had some more come out, but not much. And the then to bed, feeling tired before 10:00. Every day was an adventure and a teaching for all of us.

While watching TV that evening some talk came up about getting him some shorts and he said, "Don't worry Eleanor will take care of it." That was the first time he had mentioned her name in relation to her doing something, or even bringing her name up. She's been such a constant companion to him for the past three months there may be some sense of loss in not seeing her. If she was here that morning she probably would have convinced him there was no movie. And like Jacob mentioned and like I have felt, he may respond easier to a kind woman then to my young sons.

Miguel is making a commitment to take care of grandpa when Eleanor leaves for the Abode. It locked him into being at home, but since he was around anyway maybe it gave him a worthwhile feeling, and was helping me out and keeping it in the family.

There were a couple of possibilities for women to put in some time with dad, and I had to keep that in mind. I knew that at some point Miguel would get stir-crazy being here too often.

1533

CHAPTER 6

*Vignettes
Music And A
Dance For Dad*

MARCH 27, 1995 This was a musical weekend for dad. On Friday night we went to see my daughter Rebecca in a dance recital. It was an Isadora Duncan dance class she's been taking for the past few months. Dad had watched her in rehearsals, totally enjoying her practice classes. When she came out onto the floor for the performance, he lit up and said, "That's her," not being sure what her name was. He has said her name looking at her picture recently. He was really thrilled, with a smile on his face, watching her dance even though he probably wasn't sure who she was in relationship to him. He did seem to be more familiar with her than the rest of my children even though she is with us the least. Maybe because she's a she.

The following night there was going to be a swing dance. "Dad," I told him, "we're going to hear some music tonight. Maybe there'll be some dancing."

"Music," he responded, "who wants to hear music?"

"You like to listen to music. We heard some last week, jazz down at the plaza." I knew he didn't remember the incident, but he was usually ready to listen and watch live music.

"I like music?"

"Yeah, you do. There may be some dancing too."

"Whose going to dance?"

"I don't know. Maybe you will. You used to like to dance with mom."

"Oh yeah, dancing with mom. Whose mom? Where'd we go?"

"My mom, your wife, Mae. You used to go dancing with her at the condo, when they had entertainment at night."

"I did."

"Yeah, you did." I didn't want to get into a whole discussion, but I was trying to create some interest and again to stimulate his memory, but that always seemed useless. "Come on, we'll both have a good time. Let's get your shoes on."

"What do I need help with my shoes? I can get my shoes on." He was emphatic about that. Sometimes he managed them well, and sometimes he had socks over shoes, shoes over slippers, or any mix and match that came together for him.

We walked to his bedroom and I sat across from his bed as he took off his slippers. Then he held each shoe in his hands for a bit before deciding which foot they went on, then he put his slipper on over the front of his shoes. He looked at them a few seconds, he looked at me, then laughed. "That doesn't look right," and took off the slippers, started to take off the shoes. "No dad, leave on the shoes, we're going out dancing." He did, then tied the shoes, and said, "Okay pop, where we going?"

I was surprised he remembered we were going anyplace. Again, I reminded him, he was the father, "Dad, you're the pop, I'm the son." I know it didn't matter, but I could never let it go. "We're going to listen to some live dance music."

"I'm waiting for you pop, what's taking you so long."

When we arrived, we sat on a couple of chairs, and friends came over to say hello, dad responding with a great, big, friendly, smile. He began tapping his feet as soon as the music started, along with a rhythmic, swaying, of his body. Dad was totally taken in by the music. An Asian nurse I knew from the hospital came over to talk with us a couple of times. She was real friendly and warm with dad, and finally asked me if he could dance. "Sure I told her, he would like that." Away from him hearing, I told her he falls sometimes and had Alzheimers. As soon as she asked him to dance his hand went out to her offered hand and they walked holding hands onto the dance floor. There was a small turnout, about 20 people and none were on the dance floor so it was all theirs. She started off carefully, slow and properly as she gauged his abilities, and then began to move a bit more as he was getting the feel for her rhythm. His face took on this broad, glowing smile, his body moving a bit stiffly, but as he moved about I could see his obvious recollection of past years. I was surprised how well he was moving with her. They did two numbers in a row then she brought him back to his chair, the glowing smile still on his face.

Soon after she came back for him, not me, and led him back to the dance floor. This time the music was a bit faster and she held him closer so as to give him more support. I was surprised how close they were and I wondered if she was some kind of weird, sex freak coming on to a septuagenarian. I was asking myself with some reason.

The dance was sponsored by the Arts and Medicine Program from the hospital where we worked, so she brought some of her poetry to share, and left it right on the desk where we paid our money to get in to the dance. While standing at the desk I leafed through her poetry journal, reading very sexual references, some a bit perverse, or with confusion of what she was experiencing; all intimate and erotic. And now here she was dancing close, almost suggestively with my father. It probably didn't make much difference, except maybe I would have liked to be dancing with her myself.

She kept him going for almost half an hour off and on and he didn't mind it a bit. We stayed to the end of the 90-minute performance. He was a bit weak from his enjoyable workout, but relished every minute of it.

I felt a slight bit of pride in what I was doing with my father and with my children. To see him having a good time dancing was a thrill for me knowing we were all doing something to help a family grandfather.

Some of the guests were students from Jacob's massage school who were impressed with dad's youthful nature. A few of Jacob's classmates came up to me complimenting Jacob telling me how much they liked Jacob in the class.

It was a different kind of evening. Definitely a hit all around. When we came home I left him in his room for a few minutes and when I came back he as was laying in bed with three hats on.

"Dad, what do you have three hats on."

"I have three hats?"

"Yeah, you do."

He took one off. Looked at it and put it back on his head.

"There's that's better."

I had gotten accustomed to him sometimes going around the house or to bed with more than one hat and realized early on that it really didn't matter. I had to ask him out of curiosity, "Dad, did you like dancing with that sexy oriental woman?"

He looked at me with a kind of questioning expression. "What dance?"

That was it: Another good time with my father. Enjoying the moment and on to the next, three hats and all.

More music the next day when we went A Botanical Garden for the Spring Flower and Garden Show. There was a lot to see, but I brought dad right over to the music where he sat for the next two hours listening to country and western, square dancing, fiddling, and sat through a science experiment show. Enjoying it all. I didn't take him around to see the exhibits due to the uneven level of the ground. I also knew he preferred music.

I was very pleased with how he did all weekend. We were on the move three days, but he never complained about being tired, or not wanting to go, nor having any trouble walking, enjoying the music and the people wherever we went. What more can I ask for at this stage of his life? That was one of the wonderful things about him: Not only was he in the moment, but he enjoyed it.

I'm getting the feeling that dad doesn't know who I am. Dah, wake up Bob. No matter how many times I remind him that I'm not his father he calls me "pop." I asked him my name the other day and he said "Jacob." "No dad, my son's name is Jacob and your father's name is Jacob, but my name is Robert, your son. You took care of me with Mae your wife when I was a little boy."

"You were never a little boy," he told me.

I laughed, "yea I was dad, and you took care of me. Really. You can't remember me when I was young and you were my dad?"

He sat there. He didn't answer. He looked at me like I was lying, or a complete stranger. What could I say, again, and again? "Aah, it's okay dad. I love you even if you think I'm your dad."

GETTING UP FOR SCHOOL

MAY 4, 1995

It's Saturday. Dad woke up at seven and got dressed.

"Where you going dad?"

"To school," he told me.

"To school? What school?"

"P.S. 38."

"Where's that?"

"In the Bronx."

"How old are you?"

"18."

"18? Your not 18. And you don't have any school to go to."

"I don't. Am I out of school? Am I 19?"

I smiled at him, "Dad, your 80."

He laughed at that one. "I'm 80, how I'd get to be 80?"

"You just did dad. You've lived a long life with Mae your wife in Lauderdale Lakes for 20 years and before that in New Jersey." And again, for whatever my inner reason I try to be logical with him. "I'm your son, Robert. I'm 54 and you are 80 and my father. There's no school for you to go to so you can just lay down and sleep for another hour or so. It's Saturday and there's nothing to do for a while." Well he finally caught on and went back to bed and the incident, like everything that goes on with him, was as if it never happen.

WHOSE WHO?

After I had my breakfast, it was time to get dad up and change his diaper. When I came into his room, he was looking at the very full blooming azaleas that filled the outside of his window. "Hi, pop," he said to me, "look at my flowers."

"They're pretty dad, and they are all for you. You're lucky to have them there. I need to change your diaper. It's probably wet."

"What diaper?"

'The one you're wearing. You've had it on all night and it's probably soaked."

"Whataya talking about? I don't wear a diaper."

"Yeah, you do dad, you forget. I keep reminding you about things, but your forget as soon as I tell you."

"I do?"

"Yeah, you do." Here I'll show you the diaper you're wearing." I took off his p.j.s, showed him the diaper. He looked at it but said nothing. I got the wash cloth, wiped him, dried him off, and put on corn starch."

He looked at the yellow box, saw the word "argo" and said, "argo, argo f*** yourself. He laughed. I laughed with him. It was all part of the routine. Interesting with the memory of something he probably hasn't said in many, many decades.

I got him dressed and out in the dinning area. "Okay, want some breakfast, dad."

"Sure what you got?"

"I'll squeeze two oranges, then oats, with raisins, banana and soy milk."

"Yeah, I'll take that."

I served it up for him then told him I was going to the back yard to hang clothes on the line. Sometimes I would question my sanity hanging clothes on a line, but with all the sun, it seemed right. Then I went back in. His empty bowl and cup were in front of him. "Here, dad I'll take those away for you."

"What for?"

"You finished your breakfast. I'll wash them."

"I didn't get anything to eat yet. I'm waiting for it."

I laughed. "Dad, here's the bowl and cup from your cereal and juice."

"No it isn't. I didn't have anything yet."

He was getting a bit anxious with this exchange. I kept my voice and tempo calm and attentive: "Yeah you did. Believe me. I made it for you and put it on the table and you ate it while I was hanging stuff on the line to dry. You had a good appetite. It's a blessing. Here I am again trying to convince him of a reality that doesn't exist in his mind.

"Don't tell me I ate breakfast! I didn't have anything!" A angry, loud voice. Not 100% content.

90% Buddha-mind, 10% normal. Maybe the opposite, manifesting energy from someplace in him that has been held back. Arguing is useless. I'll get him something. "You want some tea and toast?"

"Yeah, give me tea and toast, if that's all you'll give me. They don't feed me here anyway."

"We feed you good dad. The best food we can get. Some of it right from our backyard garden. I give you peas to eat from the garden. You like them." There I go again, trying to help him remember.

"I do? You grow food here?"

"Yeah, I do dad. Here's your tea and toast. Enjoy it.

"Where you going pop?"

"I have to get ready for work.

"You work?"

"Yeah, I work at a hospital as a social worker. I have to go soon. Traci, the young black lady that stays here with you when I'm gone will be here soon then I'll leave for work. She helps take care of you."

"Help me, what kind of help do I need?"

"Anything, dad. She'll help you with food, or change your diaper, or take you out to do something. Actually today you go to Al's Place. They'll pick you up."

"The bus."

"Yes the bus." A break through, he remembers the bus. "You remember taking the bus?"

"Sure I remember the bus. Why shouldn't I remember the bus?"

"Do you know where the bus takes you?"

"No, where does it take me?"

I'm tired of it all sometimes, my patience running thin, or dry. "It doesn't matter dad. I have to get to work. Traci just pulled in the driveway and will be here with you until the bus comes. I'll see you later. One last thing: The bus takes you to the Alzheimer's Program, 'Alz Place.' I love you dad. See you later."

"I love you too pop."

Traci is has been staying with dad for the past few months. The first morning, she came in and went right to the couch, covered herself with a blanket, and made herself comfortable. Not many smiles nor very friendly. Since than though she has been attentive enough with him to satisfy me. Sometimes taking him out to her own apartment, feeding him there, or taking him when she has to run errands. On the other hand, I can come home from work and find him in soiled diapers. I remind her to please keep him changed, but it doesn't happen that way all the time.

DAD GOES FOR A SWIM

I took dad with me out to visit friends who live on a small lake. After a few of us sat talking for a while, we decided to walk down to the lake for a swim. I asked dad if he was interested, but as I expected he didn't want to go. I told him to stay on the porch and we'd be up in a while. He seemed comfortable with that plan. After we were in the lake for fifteen minutes, I looked up and see him trucking down to the lake. It wasn't a long walk, twenty-five yards or so, but on an uneven, grass covered ground, sloping to the lake, he had to move slow and carefully. I went to meet him and talked with him about what he wanted to do. In a proud, somewhat vain way, he said, as if he did this all the time, "I'm going swimming, what do you think."

Yeah, what did I think? I walked with him the rest of the way to the water. Then helped him off with his sneakers and socks, deciding not to get his bathing suit, which was in the car. I didn't want to lose the moment. I asked him if he wanted to take off his shorts and swim in is underpants, but he said, "No, I don't do that." He said he wanted to go in his shorts.

He approached the water very tentatively, with me holding his hand. He stopped at the water's edge, and began taking off his shorts, saw his underpants and pulled up on the shorts. He again said, "I don't want to swim in my underpants."

We entered the water, very, very, slowly. When the water was up to his calf, he had a hard time walking forward, and began to lean backward. At one point, me still holding his hand, his balance, and mine, were lost and we slowly went down into sitting positions. We had a good laugh sitting there. I asked him if he wanted to remain sitting in the water, but he said no, so I helped him up and we continued walking out further where the others were swimming and talking. He had this amazing, broad grin on his face during this whole episode, although he continued to be a bit uncertain about what he was doing. I asked him if he remembered how to swim. He very confidently said, "Sure, how can one forget to swim."

Actually, he was an excellent swimmer. Almost every morning for 20 years he would go to the pool in their condo and swim for 20 minutes. As a young man he used to swim in the Atlantic Ocean, long distances, paralleling the beach. As his AD took hold he went out for his daily swim less and less, and now hadn't been swimming for at least two years.

Even though he was expressing confidence in his intention, I had to keep encouraging him to move his feet forward, similarly as on dry ground.

My friend Nancy came and joined us, taking dad's other hand, and now with added support he moved further out with more certainty. After about fifteen minutes of a twenty-foot walk, we were to a point where the water was above his waist. He began pulling on our hands to let go, as he submerged his body, coming up blowing out water, beginning his stroke, one arm lifted out of the water, his other pulling underneath, his face going in on each stroke, coming out each time his arm surfaced taking a breath, his legs moving underneath, never breaking the surface with even a ripple. I walked along side of him until he was out above my neck and I told him to turn around. I wasn't sure if he heard me, with his head going in and out of the water, but he turned, continuing his stroke towards shore. Nancy remained on one side, me on the other, and once he had his rhythm, he didn't stop going in circles for about 20 minutes, except to stop occasionally to stand, look around, and then continue his stroke. Two or three times he would put his face in the water, sort of bubble underneath and come up take some air, like some kind of prehistoric sea animal, doing some kind of rest for himself. After he had his fill he started walking towards the shore. I remained by his side the whole time. Nancy had gone back with our friends.

He showed no exhaustion from his swim, but I wasn't sure if he could walk back up the sloping field to the house. I asked him if he wanted me to get the car, but he said "No, I can walk," which he did without shoes. I held onto his hand part of the way, but at some point he pulled it away from mine, not wanting or needing the support.

When we were all back on the porch, friends at the house complimented his swimming, he brushed it off as "Not much of a swim," having memories, or a sense of what he used to do or who he used to be.

A MEMORY RETURNS

Dad and I were sitting alone tonight when the both of us began to make some silly jokes, having some good laughs together. We discussed what it was like living in New Jersey, and he was able, with some prodding to recall his work at Brewery Company in Orange, N.J. and him being the shop steward for a short time. I have no idea what his 27 years in the brewery were like, but he said he was in charge of everyone and they would come to him to find out what to do.

I asked him if he remembered George Coy, a man who lived down the street from us and worked with dad. I asked him if George was a shop steward also. "He was under me," dad said.

I tried to see if he was certain with what he did: "You had men working under you?"

"Yeah, they all did."

"Weren't most of them Italians."

"No, Germans."

"Germans? You had all Germans working under you. Did they give you problems?"

"Never."

"What did you tell them to do?"

"Go hide, till there was something to do."

This was fifteen years after the World War II. I think, as a Jew, he must have had exceptional qualities about him to win the trust of these 20 or 30 Germans.

I never try and trick or deceive him of what's going on, but sometimes it felt wrong to not to try and clarify the reality with him even if it didn't make any difference to him. Time after time and it didn't get any clearer. So, I wondered who was I clarifying for? He doesn't care one way or the other. Most of the time he doesn't even know, or seem to know anything one way or the other. So is it for me to just have my say about what's going on? Seems childish or unnecessary. I tell myself I don't have to clarify for him since he doesn't care, and it doesn't matter.

Dad was a relaxed man. Everyone should have this laid back peace of being.

8/28/1995

Gabe, Becca, dad and I went to Ft. Lauderdale to visit with my mother and also see Meko and Dean, Miguel's, half brother and sister. Miguel was going to come also, but before we left I lost my temper over dishes left undone all night yelled and screamed at both Miguel and Jacob. Jacob for trying to silence me with his sweet talking logic and rationale that works in some instances, but not this time, when I knew for sure I was right and been feeling angry for some time about dishes left over during the day when I'm at work and have to clean them up or leave them as I prepare a meal and then they all go off leaving more to be cleaned up. My loud angry outburst was an over reaction, but it was in me and needed released. Maybe other anger was in me over other things, the world, Linda, my ex-wife and who knows what, but I did know that I had been bothered by the regularity of the dirty kitchen and needed it stopped. I hope my vocal violence had gotten the message across to these young men of mine.

The total trip wasn't so bad although my mother and I had our usual disagreements over this and that, but it all went fairly well, mostly because I'm used to her way, but she seemed to deal with dad a bit easier. She didn't bother him as much as usual but in general was uptight about everything. That's the way she is. I was also feeling a bit upset about what went on at home before we left, so whatever went on with her was secondary to what I was feeling about my own kids.

Actually my outburst was on my mind all weekend. I thought about it a lot trying to understand this out of character aspect of myself.

When I came home neither, Jacob or Miguel said anything about it and when I did today, telling them both that they didn't deserve my verbal wrath Jacob said he didn't think about it after it occurred but I know Miguel had it on his mind and acknowledged it, with only a word or two, but really didn't say any words he might have been thinking.

Dad peed each night we were at my mom's, but we had a plastic sheet under his bed sheet and it didn't go through to the couches mattress. Mom wasn't even too upset over the urine with the plastic cover sheet being peed on. I was expecting her to be more angry over him doing this, but she seemed to be more accepting of what his limitations were. Naturally she tried to push him to do or remember things that he wasn't able to, but she actually didn't go to far with nagging him. He did yell back at her a couple of times for her persistence, but it all seemed minor, unless I was just not being too sensitive myself to the ever present and ongoing disagreements.

He seemed to enjoy being around her, but when it was time to go he left as if she was just anybody and not his wife of 55 years. And once we were gone he made no mention of her again. And a day later he still hasn't.

9/17/95

Dad's been peeing more frequently and we have begun to put diapers on him again. We had stopped for a few days when he was using the bathroom as he needed. Jacob told me dad peed either in his bed or pants nine times in the past three days. I don't quite remember what the number is, but I've changed him a few times also. I received a homeopathic remedy today that is supposed to help with senile incontinence. I'll give it to him a few times a day for a few days and see what happens. His hernia is bulging more and maybe it is putting pressure on something or doing something that doesn't allow him to feel the need for urinating. He yelled at me last night, "WHAT DO YOU WANT ME TO DO?" when I gently complained to him about all the peeing he's been doing and how difficult it is to keep up with the changes. I told him I know it's a problem he can't control and we'll just do what we can do.

But then later I had the thought, 'what am I doing, why am I doing, can I keep this up? I've begun to wonder if I am cheating myself out of time and female affection by having my time so occupied with him. I want to do it and female affection aside, because there is no real connection between the two, him and someone. But I did realize recently that now that the boys are more independent, I should be having more time for going out and doing something about finding some female love in my life to share how really good, in general, I've been feeling about myself. I even wondered about putting him in a nursing home and what that would be like and how awful it would feel seeing him every so often with the lack attention they give. (Nur Allah was away for couple of months and here I am thinking of finding someone else. Not a great quality.) Sometimes I feel that about how we are caring for him. Me and or the boys, and how he stays with smelly pants sometimes because we don't see him pee or notice that his pants are wet. Or if he's in a diaper and he stays in it for the day and how it is soaking wet in the evening. I always give him a rag and help him clean himself when he does wet himself, and he gets a shower two times a week, so what can I do.

I don't know, except at times I'm feeling burdened by this care, and don't know whether I should get over that feeling, or whether it is something that should be naturally real to me and just learn how to live with the decision I made and feel it is the right thing to do. One morning while driving to work, just leaving the house I yelled inside the car, opened the window, "God, how much am I supposed to do?"

I took dad for an exam at our local hospital today. He was seen by Dr. John who saw him last year right about the same time. According to what John checked, dad was in okay health, but said we should try and get more fluids in him. One of the main reasons for taking him in was to have his rupture checked. I'm having the feeling it may be protruding out a bit more then last year, but it never bothers dad, but I am just being extra precautious because of his age.

The nurse, checked blood pressure, temperature, heart rate, then Dr. John came in and listened to his heart, lungs, asked a few questions and then began to check the ruptured intestine that protrudes through his abdominal wall. Dr. John felt it, measured it, rubbed round it and then began to delve deeper into and under it almost taking hold of the protuberance, acting a bit fascinated by my dad's anomaly. He then even poked his finger up into dad's scrotum area seemingly feeling for something. Well, he was thorough, but couldn't come up with anything that needed urgent attention. "Keep paying attention to it, if it becomes painful, then we can do more."

11/14/94

Another visit to Ft. Lauderdale with dad, Becca and Jacob for the first time in two or three years. Tina also came down to help celebrate our mother's 80th birthday. Unfortunately, it wasn't as much a family celebration, but more like an emotional, family fiasco.

I tend to blame our mother for us not being able to have a good time, but the fact that Tina's husband died two weeks ago also effected how Tina was feeling, although she did seem to want to have a good time. She's trying to deal with Gene's death in a very realistic way, since he was dying for the past six- months, so his final breath was not unexpected.

Tina did have the realization though, that she wasn't loving her mother. I told her that I've had that same thought many times and keep trying to undo that feeling and grant her honor for her age and being my mother. I went through that especially on this visit since it was her 80 birthday and I wanted it to be special. She doesn't seem to allow herself to feel good and Tina at one point mentioned to me, and then to her, about her not smiling. She will laugh at an obvious joke, but generally, she has a sour look on her face. I've brought it to her attention in the past, but she didn't seem to be able to change how she had become. One of the factors, excuses she uses for why she is the way she is, and it has some relevance, is that she can't remember being hugged by either of her parents. Maybe she didn't have loving parents. I'm not sure if I did. Good and caring but not so loving. Maybe that's why I left home just before my 20th birthday.

DAD NEEDS A NURSING HOME

My dad continued living with us for about a year and a half going to Alz Place three times a week. Until….They called me from Alz Place to tell me he had just sort of collapsed and complained about some pain in his hips. I think he came home on the bus, no recollection of me leaving work and going to get him. But once home he was in constant pain. I took him to the ER but he couldn't tell them exactly where the pain was so they never checked his hip, until I brought him back in to the ER after they sent him home not being thorough enough to find the pain source. He felt it though.

He knew where it was. He began swearing feeling so much pain. I took him back to the ER where he ended up having surgery on his hip the next day and was in the hospital for a couple of weeks. Here was my answer to my question to God about 'How much longer can I care for my Dad?' I knew this was more than we or I was able to handle since he would need someone helping him in and out of bed. There was no choice so he went to a nursing home not far from where I work. I actually worked in that nursing home for a short time.

I would visit him irregularly since he barely paid attention when I came to see him, although one day as he was sitting near another resident, he said, "There's my son." Wow, that was a thrill for me that he came into the present. I took him out a few times with my children but this was difficult since he wasn't able to walk well and we'd have to help him get in and out of my car using a wheel chair to get around.

I also took my mom to see him but she didn't like going into the nursing home and seeing all the 'old sick people,' as she referred to them.

Not having him at home made my life and the life of my kids much easier. Miguel left a few weeks ago but we speak on the phone occasionally.

A great incident happened when, my one uncle Don, dad's brother, came to visit. Dad was getting a shave from a nurse. He was holding the mirror in front of him when his bother came into the room. Dad saw his brother in the mirror he was holding and excitedly said, "Dad," relating his brother to their father. They had a good time visiting for a short while, since dad didn't communicate much, and Donnie had a plane to catch. The incident passed. It is remembered by me having a picture in my living room, now on the cover of this book, the three of us smiling together.

Since I didn't want to keep writing about the boring visits I had with my father in the nursing home, I'm concluding my book with this wonderful episode that happened to me in Creston, Colorado and subsequently to my father.

4313

SEEKING MY SPIRITUAL VOICE
AND THE
DEATH OF MY FATHER

My Father died recently at the age of 83. He seemed to have qualities of a Saint. I know, he's my father, so why shouldn't I see him in the highest light possible, although many people have fathers they could never say that about. This man was different. In fact, the circumstances surrounding the day of his death and the day of his burial gave it the feeling of auspiciousness. I'll share those incidents after my tale of being in Crestone.

A few weeks prior to his death I decided to go see my 31 year old son, Miguel, in Denver who thought he might have a heart problem. I hadn't seen him in over a year and needed to have a visit. He also needed a visit from me. He had been in a detox treatment and was being sober so support was something I wanted to give him. I was also burnt out on some situations in my life and needed a break.

When my friend Eyhanna heard I was going to Denver she told our mutual friend, Nur Allah, I had to visit the town of Crestone, about 3-4 hours south of Denver. I didn't know Eyhanna well but I went to visit her to find out about Creston. She was almost insistent I go there. She told me that the town and area surrounding Crestone were sacred to the Native Americans. She also described a number of spiritual centers around this town and gave me a map of where they were, plus the names of a few people to contact.

Since I felt a strong connection with Native American people and trusted my spiritual life, this felt perfect.

A few days before leaving, Eyhanna invited me to her house along with Nur Allah, who was also insistent that I visit Eyhanna before leaving.

I wasn't sure what they were up to but I casually said to a friend, "I think she is going to do some shamanistic work on me in preparation for the trip." I wasn't even sure of Eyhanna's energies. She didn't even share with me why she wanted me to visit but there was a feeling in me I didn't know how to describe, like when one is feeling pulled to be someplace. Since Nur Allah was in on what was going on I knew it could only be for the good.

It turned out Eyhanna did know a variety of shamanistic practices. When Nur Allah and I came to her house they briefly told me what Eyhanna needed to do for me.

She had me lie down on a massage table and began to do some ceremonial service over my body; there was incense burning as well as a few candles. At one point Eyhanna asked me, "What is your intention in going to Crestone?" I was slightly taken aback since she was the one who had told me to go there; primarily I was going to see Miguel in Denver.

A slight trance state had come over me while on the table from the sounds she made with Tibetan bells and rubbing a Tibetan prayer bowl with a wooden stick. She and Nur Allah also had rubbed essential oils on my hands, feet and forehead. I sensed high vibrations or energies surrounding us.

Without thinking too much of an answer to her question, some place inside of me said, "I want to find my spiritual voice." I repeated the simple phrase a few times as if instilling it in myself. It was also not in my usual speaking voice. I supposed that entreaty from a deep place inside of me was something I had been seeking for a long time. The atmosphere Eyhanna helped create around us allowed me to verbalize a deeper intention. I was very surprised that those words came out of me.

When the two-hour session was over there was a sense in me I had been on a journey. It had been a journey, one of mind, body and spirit. My physical journey was to begin in two days.

While sitting in the Orlando airport my thoughts dwelled on my Father, especially how weak he appeared in the nursing home the past two weeks. My dad had Alzheimer's Disease for the past six year, but always maintained a friendly, smiling demeanor about him to all those who knew him. That was his trademark nature his whole life. Except at times when his dementia became too dominant. During my last visit with him, at the nursing home, my mother had to feed him because he was too weak or disinterested. He barely wanted anything to eat but my mother kept prodding him, and eventually, he did eat most of the nursing home food. We also heard a lot of congestion his lungs so I asked the nurse on staff to have a doctor check him out. As my mother and I left him, I told her, "Mom, I think we can expect anything at this point."

Then while sitting on the plane before take off I asked myself, what would I do if he died while being in Colorado. Until then there was never the serious thought of him dying, but after my visit to him, something in me felt this might be the case.

Odd, but death in one form or another was on my mind since the morning before going to the airport. It was odd of me to question myself about what I would do if he died while I was away. Something felt it would be complicated being with Miguel and having to arrange for us both to come back to Florida if he did die.

I arrived in Denver on a Friday and spent a great weekend with Miguel and his lady friend Vonnie. It was a good relief to hang out with him this way rather than our time together in Gainesville when he was helping care for my father. My time alone in a motel was in meditation and reading a book by Sufi Master, called, That Which Transpires Behind that Which Appears. This is a book about being on a spiritual retreat. This wasn't my initial plan in going to Crestone, but as it turned out, that's what was planned for me.

A few weeks previously I joked with Nur Allah about her going on spiritual retreats and how so many others we knew were doing the same. "I don't get that opportunity very often even as my life was moving forward. Maybe I'm needing a spiritual retreat." Thanks to Nur Allah and Ehyanna, my visit to Miguel turned into that and much more.

Before I left Denver for Crestone, Miguel asked me, "Where are you going to stay and what are you going to do there?"

"I've no clue It's all a matter of trust and faith, Miguel. I'm feeling open and receptive." When I look back at this Crestone adventure, as I wrote above, it was obvious, as sometimes happens–it was all laid out for me before hand. I have known there has been extraordinary synchchronicity in my life. I am thankful.

I rented a car and Monday morning left for Crestone with no expectations. That's been a good quality of mine, not to have expectations, but to try and be positive about what life can bring to me. My drive was exhilarating and wonderful. It excited me seeing the broad spacious vistas and snow peaked Rocky Mountains I hadn't seen in 20 years.

I arrived in Crestone early in the afternoon. After making some inquiries I was soon making my way up the road to the area where some of spiritual centers were located that Ehyanna had told me about. My first stop was a Carmelite Center for Catholic renunciates. There was a sign on their road they were on their own retreat, so I just walked around the grounds admiring the unique design.

Then drove further up the long bumpy dirt road to the Ashram honoring Babaji, the Avatar Paramahansa Yogananda writes about in the Autobiography of a Yogi. There was one man on the premises who simply told me I could go into the temple if I liked. It was a very small, beautifully designed temple, with a glorious alter depicting the Divine Mother and pictures I assumed of Babaji in his last incarnation. I only stayed there a short time, 15 minutes, since my knees were hurting sitting cross legged and there were no chairs for me to sit on. When I came out the man who spoke to me earlier, who was from Italy, showed me around a bit.

I could see that many hands had worked on the Ashram. There was a beautifully designed solar building used as a kitchen, a work area, plant nursery, business area for helping promote and distribute materials regarding Babaji as well as related sacred objects. There were other work projects going on around the small compound. The Italian man invited me to come back the following day to talk with the woman who was managing the facility and see if I could sleep on a futon he showed me. I thanked him for the hospitality and left to see what else awaited me.

As I drove still further up the same unpaved road there was a sense of some reminiscent enjoyment of other rural roads I enjoyed driving on, especially those few years in Arkansas and West Virginia where I was part of communal living. Then I came to the Crestone Mountain Zen Center and Lindesfarne Chaple. Here again only one person was on the premises. He told me the residents of the Zen Center were on a retreat. They were not taking guests for two weeks, but I could look around and visit the Zendo if I wished. With all these renunciates on retreat it felt like a perfect time for me to be on a retreat of my own.

I bypassed the Zendo being drawn to the wonderfully constructed Lindesfarne Chapel which was built by the previous owners of the property. A plaque on the side of the Chapel said the owners were a professional group of seekers who had built the Chapel as a special place of worship with the intention to bring peace and love to earth.

Before entering I instinctively took off my shoes feeling I was entering a place of sacredness. Upon entering I was immediately entranced, taken in by the sacred sense of the space. The Dome was about 60 feet in diameter and about 20 feet high at its peak. There was an exquisite structural design across the top created by architects who knew exactly what they were doing. There was also only one place for light to come into the Dome. This was at the apex of the dome. Around the circumstance of the Dome, on the floor, there was a two-foot wide two-foot high sitting ledge with 12 sitting places equidistant apart all with backrests,

There was a feeling of specialness inside of me having been guided to this place. I proceeded respectfully when entering not going in very far at first, but was simply drawn to sit on the first seat to my left near the door.

As I sat and meditated, wondering if the 12 sitting places were for the 12 Disciples of Christ. It felt an honor to be there and began to chant Om Shanti Om a number of times in harmony with the purpose of peace the Dome represented. In return my ears heard a wonderful resonance echo. The design was perfect.

After sitting for 30 minutes I was moved to walk to the center. There, in the center, were two large circular flat stones one on top of the other; they were about five to six inches thick and five to eight feet around. I took them to be an Alter. On the top was a candle and matches in the center. The Altar was a three hundred year old millstone from San Luis, the oldest town in Colorado. (When I returned home Eyhanna told me the stones were brought there by Native Americans.)

After contemplating the stones for a few minutes a deep sense within me began doing a sacred walk around the stones. My walk was slow, deliberative and meditative. Soon my circle expanded, continuing to expand until I was walking the full circumference of the chapel. As I walked a chant I love came out of me, "Our Earth is Our Mother, We Must Take Care of Her."

Then my walk contracted back to the center, close again to the sacred stones, then once again, expanded to the outer circumference. There was no clue in me why this was happening, except following an inner guide that intuitively felt the sacredness of the space.

After an hour in the Dome I left feeling totally entranced. I wanted to find Marshall the man who invited me to look around. Something in memory reminded me of meeting him in Costa Rica, but he was no-where to be found. I walked to the Zendo but the door was locked. This was okay with me since the austere meditation done in a Zendo always felt a bit stringent for me. The Dome had offered me more than I knew or expected.

As it was getting towards evening I realized I needed to find a place to sleep. Driving back towards town I passed a small stream where I stopped for a few minutes to make a tobacco offering which Eyhanna had asked me to do for her. I did this three times in my four days in Crestone—for her, for the earth and myself. I also made prayers of gratitude for the opportunity to be in this place. (At the time I used to roll American Spirit organic tobacco.)

While continuing down the mountain there was a pleasant surprise when I saw about 20 deer come out of the woods and graze near the road. What a sight! I stopped the car to watch them serenely continue their business as I sat only a few feet from them. Other cars passed by as the drivers gave the deer little attention as the deer did the same to the cars. I surmised that since the area did not allow shooting guns within a mile outside the town limits the deer knew this was protected area for them. After having my fill of what was, I supposed, a common occurrence, I drove on.

Once in town I called one of the phone numbers Ehyanna had given me for a possible bed and breakfast. They weren't in business but the man gave me a phone number of another b and b that did have accommodations. Auspiciousness! auspiciousness! I stayed there for four nights enjoying myself with wonderful spiritually minded couple that provided a perfect place for my retreat.

It was well after dark when I came to the b and b. After they showed me the room I went to bed with a bad headache, which wasn't common for me. Awakening during the night it was still there, in the morning the same. It finally went away after my meditation as I focused my energy on clearing away the headache.

In the morning after muffins and tea and getting to know my hosts, I sat in their driveway enjoying the May sun and the panoramic view of the 14,000 foot snow covered peaks of the Sangre de Cristo (Blood of Christ) mountains to the north and the tens of thousand of acres of the San Luis Valley in the west. Then my hostess, Judith, came out of the house and invited me to sit on their patio and get a still better view of the mountains. As I sat reading and contemplating, my hosts came out occasionally to further get acquainted. I enjoyed them right away and was pleased they were so friendly. Later, Dennis, the husband, came out with a special crystal that a friend of theirs had recently given them. They were told it wasn't actually a crystal, but crystal-like, called Andara, composed of something called Prima Matra. The written material Dennis and Judith were given was extensive. Briefly: "As the earth condensed from a pure spiritual state into the first states of matter, Prima Matra formed from the ether. Since that time there have always been inner plane orders that ensured there would always be a certain amount of some form of this Prima Matra present within this dimension in order to maintain the bridge from this reality back to our true spiritual heritage. This substance is being revealed at this time to the planet to assist the Children of Light with the transformation process."

Well, I had no idea what that was all about and neither did my hosts who were only given the crystal and information a few days previously. I'm a skeptic, but like to believe there is more going on than our material world reveals to us. The more of it I read about the Andara the less I understood. What could be said about it all except, I was ready to accept what was being offered. I held the Andara for an hour looking at the sun and mountains through it, as well as putting it on parts of my body needing attention.

It was early afternoon and I felt being called for some exploration. The area outside of Crestone where the Bed and Breakfast was located is called Baca Grande. It has about 3,500 home sites, with only 300 homes built, or partially built. The land had been cleared and planned a few years ago by a retired military man. He and his wife built their own home on it. The story goes that while the wife was home one day a Native American came to their door with a medicine pipe telling her they had been waiting for them for a long time. He told her the whole area was considered sacred grounds by the Native Americans. It was a place where there was no fighting between tribes. It was now up to the new owners of the land to preserve the land for sacred purposes.

Apparently the wife, at one point, even had a vision of the burning bush, as did Moses. She invited Bill Moyers to share her vision on one of his shows. Part of the visions of the Native People included inviting spiritual groups and socially conscious organizations to use these lands for the benefit of humankind. This is all in the process of happening as I shared in my walk by the various religious retreat centers.

I decided to walk up towards the Sangre de Cristo Mountains to get a better feel for the area along with a wider view of the San Luis Valley. I walked the dirt streets, wandered off into the woods, appreciating the Aspen trees. There was curiosity in me about why all the housing sites had underground electricity and sewage but only a few with current construction in progress. There were very few finished homes.

My inner compass lead me to the base of the much higher mountains. Finally I came to what was the last street before higher elevations began. It wasn't my nature to question why my feet were taking me to this place but again, something to do with allowing all nature to lead me. At the end of the road, to my surprise, there was a chain-link like fence with barbed wire on top surrounding a building site. There was a plastic cover over the top of what must have been a foundation. One plastic drainage pipe came up through the plastic. All of this looked strange and incongruous compared to the other building sites. I walked around the fence, finding a perfect place to sit on the earth. It was the most beautiful panoramic view of the valley I could have imagined. To my back there were snow covered mountain peaks adding to the beauty of the area. The view was enthralling, enrapturing. I knew this is why I had come to this place.

I became captivated by the grandeur of where my life's path had brought me. I began to chant, pray, do affirmations of my life's purpose. This momentum went on and on then a voice came out of me that took on a different tone other than what I had known as mine. There was no way for me to know why, but this voice coming out of me, sounded vaguely, similar to the voice of Paramahansa Yogananda I had heard recently on a tape.

I remembered Eyhanna asking me about my intention and what I had told her, asking for the 'voice of my spirit to come through without being blocked by the physical body.' My feet raised me from the sitting position on the ground as my arms went up in supplication to the heavens, to God, Creator off all that is. To the spirits I felt were surrounding me. What was I? Who was I? All was lost in those moments of other beingness. One of the passages in the book by Pir Vilayat was 'that we needn't take all our past into the future.' We can become more than who we have been. During those few moments, there was an inner feeling, an experience, of something beyond myself.

Then something happened. It was very brief. From the corner of my eye about 50 to 100 yards away, through the trees, a pure white, round, smooth, oblong object, a few feet in length sped along and was quickly gone behind the mountain. I spun around, looking all around, up into the mountains. "What was that? Where did you go? Come on don't tease me. I need to see more. I want to believe." I joked a line from a very old Saturday Night live skit, "What the hell was that?" Maybe I'll never know. Maybe I do know. The thought of the Andara having been formed from an implosion caused by the Lemurians trying to manifest a black hole from the third into the sixth dimension (whatever that means). Did the object come from another dimension? It didn't come from in front of me. Where did it come from? I laughed out loud to myself, "What the hell was that?" Again and again I turned all around looking up towards the Sangre de Cristo for another sign. Nothing. That was it! I wanted a sign. I had a sign. What it meant only the Great Unknown could tell me.

A few days later I was back in Denver planning my return to Gainesville for my father's funeral. Yes, as I had thought so it occurred. Miguel had received a call and called me while I was still in Crestone. I wondered a long time whether the mysterious flying object the first evening of my father's transition had something to do with his passing from this realm. It was going west to east, in his direction. Was it an angel going for him? At the speed it appeared to be going it certainly wouldn't take four days to get to Florida, although time and space have nothing to do with this sort of energy.

There I was on this mountain praying to God, to Life, to All that is. Does God, this Life make these kind of special appearances? Of course. Before I left for my trip Nur Allah, after watching the Ten Commandments during Passover and Easter, told me, "You might see a burning bush." Was this a modern version of a burning bush? This was something very, very special.

Upon returning to the b and b I told my new friends about my experience. They told me, "This sort of thing is not uncommon. There have been many sightings of UFOs in the area."

It didn't feel what I saw was the usual kind of UFO sighting. But what is a usual UFO sighting? To me, a miracle occurred as I chanted.

Then I was in Denver having to make plans for Miguel and me to return to Gainesville. It was a full moon, Saturday, May 4th, 1996, which is celebrated as Wesak in the Himalayas. And Miguel's birthday was the May 9th. Supposedly on Wesak, is when Jesus and Buddha come together in the mountains, someplace in India, in order to fuse their energies and the energies of other high beings for the good of humanity and the planet.

Back in Gainesville for the funeral, the Rabbi told me that day was a very auspicious day in Judaism. It was the only day considered joyous in a period of 49 days between two Jewish holidays that were mostly days of somber thoughts.

Cool for you Dad. You died on a special day, full moon and Wesak, and you were buried on a special day in our religion.

What's interesting to me about the synchronicity of his death on the annual meeting of those two great beings and his burial day is celebrated also in Judaism. Added to this is that sometimes my children and I used to playfully refer to my father as being the Buddha, because of his balanced, caring, smiling, nature, living in the present with no regrets of the past and no worries for the future. This was part of his nature before he developed dementia. Now wouldn't that be something that because of his special nature he was being summoned by astral energies for the betterment of humanity. I pray it be so.

Today, June 2, 2018 I'm about finished with this account of caring for my father. Yesterday I committed myself to walk to the cemetery where both of my parents are buried. A very somber visit. Fortunately, my somberness doesn't stay with me. Blessings on both my mom and father.

Printed in the United States
By Bookmasters